London

VICKY SHIPTON

Level 2

Series editors: Andy Hopkins and Jocelyn Potter

Pearson Education Limited

Edinburgh Gate, Harlow,
Essex CM20 2JE, England
and Associated Companies throughout the world.

ISBN-13: 978-1-405-83351-6
ISBN-10: 1-405-83351-3

This edition first published by Penguin Books 2006

3 5 7 9 10 8 6 4 2

Text copyright © Vicky Shipton 2006
Map by Martin Sanders

Typeset by Graphicraft Limited, Hong Kong
Set in 11/14pt Gill Sans Light
Printed in China
SWTC/02

Produced for the Publishers by
Graphicraft Productions Limited, Dartford, UK

Published by Pearson Education Limited in association with
Penguin Books Ltd, both companies being subsidiaries of Pearson Plc

Acknowledgements

Every effort has been made to trace the copyright holders and we apologise in advance for an
unintentional omissions. We would be pleased to insert the appropriate acknowledgement in any
subsequent edition of this publication.

We are grateful to the following for permission to reproduce photographs:

Alamy: pg11 (Robert Harding), pg13 (Popperfoto), pg23 (Pictures Colour Library); **Corbis:** pg9
(Tim Graham); **FotoLibra:** pg17 (Mark Johnson); **Nicholas Armitt Photography:** pg20
(Photographers Direct); **Rex:** pg4 (Alisdair Macdonald), pg6 (John Stephen), pg15 (Tony Larkin),
pg19 (Nils Jorgenen); **TopFoto:** pg24 (Professional Sport)

Picture Research by Angela Anderson and Alison Prior

For a complete list of the titles available in the Penguin Readers series please write to your local
Pearson Education office or to: Penguin Readers Marketing Department, Pearson Education,
Edinburgh Gate, Harlow, Essex, CM20 2JE

Contents

Introduction

More than 25% of the people in London were not born there. People come to the capital from other areas of Britain. Many people come from other countries ... Today, people from many countries live in every area of the city. You can hear more than 250 languages on the streets of London, and the city is changing all the time.

When somebody says 'London', what do you think of? Old buildings? The River Thames? Red London buses? Rain? You can see all of these things in Britain's largest city. But London is really a great city because of its people. There are more than 7,000,000 Londoners. Some people say that London is 'the world in one city'.

Read this book and learn about the city's people and its buildings, about past times and the city today. This is the story of London.

Vicky Shipton was born in the United States. She moved to Turkey when she was 21. Two years later, she moved to Britain. She loves Britain, but she really loves London. She worked in the centre of the city for five years, but she didn't live there. Every day, she took a bus or a train into the great city. Now, after ten years back in the US, she is in Britain again. She lives in Cambridge, but goes to London often.

A Great City

London, in the south-east of Britain, is one of the great cities of the world. At more than 1,500 square kilometres, it is the biggest city in Europe. It is also an old city, with a long and interesting story.

How much do you know about this great city? How many of these questions can you answer? The answers are all in this book.

1 What is the tallest building in London?
a a church   b an office building   c a palace

2 What destroyed most of the city in 1666?
a a fire   b a war   c strong winds

3 How many bridges are there across the River Thames?
a eleven   b twenty   c thirty-four

4 Who – or what – is Big Ben?
a a clock   b a bell   c a king

5 Which Roman first came to the south of England?
a Claudius   b Julius Caesar   c Nero

6 Who said, 'When a man is tired of London, he is tired of life'?
a Samuel Johnson   b Charles Dickens
c William Shakespeare

7 What is Harrods?
a a restaurant   b a park   c a shop

8 Which king lost his head in 1649?
a Charles I   b Charles II   c Henry VIII

9 When did the city's first museum open?
a 1598   b 1753   c 1820

10 How many rooms are there in Buckingham Palace?
a 600   b 400   c 200

The Thames

The River Thames runs through the centre of London from west to east. Its name comes from an old word for *river*. The city is a great capital city because of this river. In past times, the Thames was a great road of water. This 'road' brought people to London, and by the 1700s it brought things from round the world – tea, sugar, wood and a lot of money. The Thames was always a busy river.

For 1,700 years, London only had one bridge – London Bridge. The first London Bridge was wood. Londoners finished a new, stone London Bridge in 1209. This stood for 622 years. It was not only a bridge. It had shops, and some people lived on it. The bridge was very busy.

A long way from home

The next London Bridge stood for 140 years. Now it is in Arizona, in the United States! In 1968 people built a new London Bridge, and the city sold the old bridge to an American. Robert McCulloch bought it for $2,460,000 and moved it to Arizona. Some Londoners say that McCulloch bought the wrong bridge. They say that he really wanted Tower Bridge!

Londoners built a second bridge across the Thames in 1750 at Westminster. By the year 1819, there were five bridges across the river. They changed life in the city. Before that, not many people lived south of the river, but now they could easily go across the Thames.

Today, there are thirty-four bridges. The most famous is east of the city centre, near the Tower of London. Workers finished

Tower Bridge in 1894. The road across the bridge goes up in the centre when big ships come through. The bridge is one of the most famous places in London. You can go on high walkways at the top of the bridge and visit a museum there.

The river helped London in many ways, but it also brought problems. For years, people threw things into it. The city's toilets ran into the river, too. The river was very dirty and its water was dangerous. By the 1950s, there were no fish. Today, things are different. The water is cleaner, and fish swim in the Thames again.

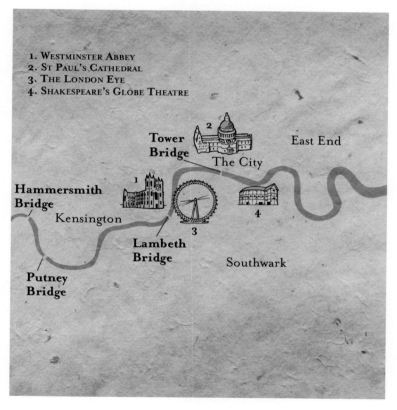

1. WESTMINSTER ABBEY
2. ST PAUL'S CATHEDRAL
3. THE LONDON EYE
4. SHAKESPEARE'S GLOBE THEATRE

The River Thames runs through the centre of the city.

The Story Begins

There were people in the area near the River Thames a long time before the Roman Julius Caesar arrived in Britain in 55 BC*. Caesar and his men fought the people in the south of the country, and Caesar said the famous words, '*Veni, vidi, vici.*' ('I came, I saw, I won.') Some people think that Caesar built the first bridge across the river.

The Romans came to Britain again eighty-eight years later. The River Thames was important to them, and they started to build a town there, north of the river. They gave it the name Londinium. (The name 'London' comes from this Roman name.) Fifteen years later, Londinium was a busy, important place.

Queen Boudica

But there were problems. In 60 AD, the Romans started a fight with the wrong person. After her husband died, Boudica, a queen in the east of the country, was angry with the Romans. She and her followers fought the Romans. They started a great fire and destroyed most of Londinium. But the Romans built the city again and it was bigger and better.

* BC/AD: years before/after Christ

By the year 100 AD, London was the capital of Roman Britain. A hundred years later, the Romans built thick city walls round Londinium. Between 20,000 and 50,000 people lived inside these walls. You can see some of the stones of the old Roman walls today.

When the Romans left Britain in 410, the good times ended. But then Saxons came to Britain from an area in Germany, and they started living near the river. In the early days, the Saxons did not use the old city, but in 834 Vikings from Scandinavia started to destroy other towns and cities. In 886, the Saxon king, Alfred, moved his people inside the old Roman city walls of Londinium.

'London Bridge is Falling Down'

Many British children sing this famous song, but not everybody knows the story. When the Vikings took London in 1013, the English king, Aethelred, asked King Olaf of Norway for help. Olaf's men pulled London Bridge down when the Vikings were on it. The bridge and the Vikings fell into the river.

In 1050 another king, Edward I, started building a great church, Westminster Abbey, west of the city. The king built a palace, Westminster Palace, between the abbey and the river because he wanted to watch the builders. Workers finished the building in 1065, and Edward died days later.

In 1066, a new king of England, William I from France, stood in Westminster Abbey. William and his son, William Rufus, started to build fine new buildings in the city. The city was now about 1,000 years old. With its new centre in Westminster, it was ready for the next 1,000 years.

King Henry III built a new Westminster Abbey two hundred years later. You can see this great building in Westminster today.

London Theatre

London is one of the theatre capitals of the world. Most of the big theatres are in the 'West End'. There are more than fifty theatres in this area. *The Mousetrap*, by Agatha Christie, started in the West End in 1952 and you can see the same play today!

A lot of the big plays in London now have songs and music in them. Some – *The Lion King, Mary Poppins* and *Billy Elliot* – were films first. One of the biggest names in London theatre is Andrew Lloyd Webber. He wrote the music for *Cats* and *Evita*.

In the 1500s, important people in the church did not like the theatre, so there were no theatres inside London's city walls. James Burbage built the first theatre, outside the walls, in 1576. Twenty-one years later, Peter Smith started building the Globe Theatre south of the river, in Southwark. This was the biggest theatre in London, and a lot of Londoners saw plays there. The first play at the Globe was about the Roman Julius Caesar. William Shakespeare (1564–1616) is Britain's most famous writer. He lived in London for most of his life, and Londoners saw most of his thirty-seven plays at the Globe.

Boys and girls

In Shakespeare's time, women could not be in plays. The people in the plays were all men. The film *Shakespeare in Love* was about this. Men played Juliet in *Romeo and Juliet* and Ophelia in *Hamlet*!

The first Globe Theatre closed in 1642, and builders destroyed it later. In the 1970s an American, Sam Wanamaker, wanted to build the theatre again. After thirty years and a lot of money, the Globe is now in its old place in Southwark. You too can see a Shakespeare play at the Globe!

Kings and Queens in London

The story of London is also the story of the country's kings and queens. Some of the most famous buildings tell this story.

The Tower of London

In 1066 the new king, William I, built the White Tower in the city. Later kings and queens built more buildings round this tower. The Tower of London was a palace, but it was also a prison. Two of King Henry VIII's wives – Anne Boleyn and Catherine Howard – lost their heads at the Tower in the 1500s. The Tower was a prison again in the 1940s: in World War II, the British government put German Rudolf Hess there. Today, visitors can walk round the Tower of London. The treasures of many kings and queens are inside.

Hampton Court Palace

Hampton Court Palace was a great house to the south-west of the city. It was Thomas Wolsey's house, but King Henry VIII liked it. Henry was angry with Wolsey. Wolsey gave the house to the king, but it did not help him. The king took the house and Wolsey went to prison. Henry changed the palace and built new gardens, kitchens and a church. Twenty-eight people could use the palace's toilet at the same time!

Later, Hampton Court Palace was a prison for King Charles I. In 1649, Oliver Cromwell's government cut off the king's head.

Parks for Kings

Many of London's parks were gardens for kings and queens. Londoners could walk in Hyde Park and St James's Park for the first time in the 1600s.

Queen Elizabeth II and her family outside Buckingham Palace

Buckingham Palace

No king or queen built Buckingham Palace. It was a rich person's house. King George III liked it and he bought it in 1761. George IV built more and more rooms. Queen Victoria moved to Buckingham Palace in 1837. Now Queen Elizabeth II lives in Buckingham Palace when she is in London. There are 600 rooms. Visitors can see some of the rooms for one month every year.

Kensington Palace

William III built this beautiful small palace 'in the country' in 1689. Later, Queen Victoria was born there. Today, the palace is in a park, near the centre of London. Some people in the Queen's family have flats in the palace.

9

East and West

London is home to about 7,200,000 people. The same number of people lived in the city in 1900. At that time, it was the biggest city in the world.

But homes in London are very different. Many of the city's richest areas are in the west of the city – in Kensington and Knightsbridge. In 2001, somebody sold the most expensive house in the city, near Kensington. They wanted £85,000,000 for it!

Of course, it is very different in other areas of the city. In the 1700s and 1800s, people built many houses east of the old city walls. In this area, the East End, most people did not have much money. The houses were small, and sometimes more than one family lived in the same house. They used the same kitchen and outside toilet.

World War II destroyed many of the houses in the East End. After the war, the British government pulled down more of these houses. They started building tall buildings for the people in the area.

Listen to the bells!

Some Londoners are 'Cockneys'. This is a name for people from one area of the East End. Cockneys are born near the sound of Bow Bells – the bells of one church, St Mary-le-Bow, in Cheapside.

More than 25% of the people in London were not born there. People come to the capital from other areas of Britain. Many people come from other countries. There are Chinese people in London's Chinatown, in the Soho area. People from India, Pakistan and Bangladesh came to the East End after World War II. In the

1950s, many people moved from the West Indies to the area of Notting Hill in west London. Every August there is a big street party in Notting Hill with Caribbean music.

Today, people from many countries live in every area of the city. You can hear more than 250 languages on the streets of London, and the city is changing all the time. From 1993 to 2002, 726,000 people from other countries moved to London. Today, a lot of people come from countries in the east of Europe. London really is 'the world in one city'.

Colour on a summer day in the streets of Notting Hill

London's Ups and Downs

There were good times and bad times in the long story of London.

⬇ **1348** A very bad illness hit the people of London. Half of all Londoners died.

⬆ **1558–1603** Elizabeth I was queen. At this time – in 'Elizabethan England' – the country's capital city was rich and strong, with more and more people and more and more buildings.

⬆ **1605** Guy Fawkes and his friends did not want James I to be king, so they tried to destroy the government building at Westminster. The government caught and killed them. Today British people remember this day, November 5th, with parties and fires in their gardens.

⬇ **1649** War began in 1642. Oliver Cromwell and his followers won, and in 1649 they killed King Charles I. After the King lost his head, there was no king or queen from 1649 to 1660.

⬆ **1660** When Oliver Cromwell died, there was a new king. Charles II was the son of Charles I. Londoners could dance and go to the theatre again.

⬇ **1665–6** Illness came to London again. At the end of 1665, 80,000 Londoners were dead. The King and many rich people left the city, so they did not die.

⬇ **1666** A fire started on a hot September day in a shop near London Bridge. In six days, the Great Fire of London destroyed most of the old city. When it ended, 100,000 Londoners had no home.

⬆ **1666** After the fire, the people of London started to build their city again. Christopher Wren (1632–1723) built some of the city's most beautiful and famous buildings. St Paul's Cathedral was one of his buildings.

⬆ **1851** Queen Victoria was queen from 1837 to 1901. The world changed in the 1800s and Queen Victoria's London was the world's biggest, richest city. There were big new train stations, museums and many other fine buildings. In 1851, there was a great show at Crystal Palace. It showed the best of British things. Queen Victoria and her husband Albert opened the show. They went forty-two times! More than 6,000,000 other people went, too.

⬇ **1941** World War II (1939–1945) was a difficult time for London. The city lost many of its houses and famous buildings in the war. After the war, London had to start again. But the people of London were ready – in 1948, the Olympic Games came to the city. The Olympics are coming again in 2012.

⬆ **Today** London is changing. People are putting a lot of money into areas near the river. Old buildings are coming down or changing. There are new offices, shops, restaurants and flats.

Many Londoners lost their homes and shops in World War II.

Old and New

There are many old buildings in London, but there are new buildings in London's story, too.

New Buildings

Telecom Tower was new in 1965. The tower was for television and radio, but it also had a restaurant at the top. The restaurant closed in 1970.

Canada Tower is London's tallest building. It is also the tallest office building in Europe. It has a red light at the top, so aeroplanes can see it.

A meat company, OXO, built the **OXO Tower** by the river in 1928. At that time, companies could not write their names in lights on the city's buildings. But the builders had an idea. They wrote the word OXO in the windows at the top of the building. Then they put a strong light behind the windows, so people outside could read the word. Today there is a restaurant at the top of the tower.

The **London Eye** is not a building, but it is the fourth tallest thing in the London sky. From the top of the London Eye, visitors can see for kilometres across the city. You go up and down again in twenty minutes.

Old Buildings

The Great Fire of London, in 1666, destroyed the old church of St Paul's. The government asked Christopher Wren for a new church. He started **St Paul's Cathedral** in 1675. In 1707, when he was seventy-five, two towers went on the building. With its round top, St Paul's Cathedral is one of London's most beautiful buildings.

People round the world know **Big Ben**. It stands next to the British government buildings at Westminster. But Big Ben is not the name of the clock or the tower. It is the name of the bell inside St Stephen's Tower. Builders finished the bell tower in 1858, but there were problems. After two months, Big Ben broke. Later, in 1949, the bell sounded four and a half minutes late because there were a lot of birds on the clock. On January 1st 1962, the clock was slow again because there was snow on it. It also stopped in 2005. For British people, the New Year starts when they hear the sound of Big Ben in the streets of London or on their televisions or radios.

The British fought Napoleon's ships in 1805 and won. The city wanted to remember this, so in 1841 they built **Trafalgar Square**. Today, you can find a lot of visitors – and birds! – in the square.

Old and New – the London Eye looks down on Big Ben's tower.

Shop, Shop, Shop!

People could always buy things in London. Today, there are about 40,000 shops in the city. Visitors can buy everything in London. Many of the city's most famous shops are in Knightsbridge or Regent Street, and some shops in these areas are very expensive. The city also has a lot of old shops.

Fortnum & Mason William Fortnum and Hugh Mason opened their shop in 1707. Later, other Fortnums and Masons worked there. They sold food in Britain and sent it to other countries, too. Now the shop sells expensive food, clothes and other things. Charles Fortnum worked for King George III in the 1700s, and today the Queen is one of the shop's customers.

Harrods This is one of the most famous shops in the world. Henry Charles Harrod started selling tea in the 1800s, when Harrods was a family shop. By 1905, Harrods was in a new building and it was the biggest shop in Europe. In 1985 the Egyptian Mohamed Al Fayed bought it. Now you can buy cakes, coffee, flowers, games, jackets, jeans, radios, shirts, shoes, telephones, televisions, vegetables, watches, toilet paper and coats for dogs! Harrods sells everything for everybody.

Liberty Arthur Liberty opened his shop in 1875. He called the building East India House, and the shop sold beautiful things from India, Japan and other countries in the East. Liberty moved to a beautiful new building in the 1920s. Now the shop is famous for its clothes.

You can also go shopping outside in London. The city has about eighty markets.

One of London's biggest markets is on **Petticoat Lane**. Every Sunday, people sell clothes to shoppers.

Portobello Road runs through the middle of Notting Hill, in the west of the city. In 1870, people sold horses on Portobello Road. Now more than 2,000 people sell clothes, music, and fruit and vegetables there.

For 300 years, **Covent Garden** was a market for fruit, vegetables and flowers. Now it is not really a market. It has a lot of different shops and restaurants. Visitors can watch street theatre in the square outside.

When Londoners are hungry, and tired of shopping, they can go to one of the 11,000 eating places in the city. You can eat food from round the world. You can eat in famous, very expensive restaurants or in cheap little cafés. In the afternoon, you can have 'afternoon tea' – tea, sandwiches and cake – in one of the city's famous hotels.

A child enjoys his visit to Covent Garden.

Museums

London has a lot of museums. There are museums of money, animals, time, trains, ships, the River Thames, tea and coffee, art, famous writers, war, buses and trains, aeroplanes, theatre – everything! The Museum of London is a museum about London!

The British Museum was the first museum in the world. In 1753, when Sir Hans Sloane died, the British government bought 80,000 of his books and other things. From 1759, everybody could go and see them in the new museum.

Today, the British Museum has over 4,000,000 things. A visitor can walk about four kilometres through ninety-four rooms. About 1,200 people work in the museum, and every year there are 6,000,000 visitors. What can they see there?

- The Lindow Man is about 2,000 years old. They found him under the ground in the north of England, in 1984. How did he die? Nobody knows.
- The Sutton Hoo treasure is the treasure of an English king of about 600 AD. This treasure tells us about life at that time.
- When people wanted to understand the old language of the Egyptians, the Rosetta Stone helped them.
- One dead cat from Egypt is more than 2,000 years old!
- Stones from the Parthenon, in Athens, came to London in 1801. Many Greek people want to take this art back to Greece.

One of the most famous areas of the British Museum is the Reading Room. At different times, many famous writers and thinkers worked here – Karl Marx, Mahatma Gandhi, Virginia Woolf and Oscar Wilde. Today, you can go to the Reading Room and learn more about the things in the museum from computers.

Of course, you can see a lot of art in London. One of the most famous museums is the Tate. The first Tate building opened in 1897 with art from the 1500s to 1890.

But the old museum building was too small, so now there are two Tates in London. The new Tate museum opened in the year 2000, by the River Thames. There is art of the 1900s, with work by Picasso, Matisse and Warhol. The old Tate museum is now 'Tate Britain'.

There are many fine treasures in the Victoria and Albert Museum.

Some of London's biggest and best museums are in Kensington. One of these is the Victoria and Albert Museum. It opened in 1852 under a different name. Students could come here and see treasures from different areas of the world. In 1899, after her husband died, Queen Victoria gave this museum its new name. Today, the museum has more than eleven kilometres of rooms. In one room you can see hundreds of dresses from 1600 to today.

Black Taxis, Red Buses

London has five airports in or near the city – Heathrow, Gatwick, London City Airport, Stansted and Luton. Heathrow is twenty-four kilometres from the city centre. About 1,250 aeroplanes – 213,000 people – fly to and from Heathrow every day.

The city has eight big train stations, too. You can catch a train from London to Paris or Brussels now. Many people live outside London and come into the city for work every day. Children know about King's Cross station because it is the train station in the Harry Potter books.

London is famous for its black taxis and red buses.

There are a lot of cars in London, and journeys can take a very long time at the wrong time of day. But the city is famous for its black taxis and red buses. You can see some of London's famous red buses today, and there are other buses, too. London's 21,000 black taxi drivers have to remember 25,000 streets in London. They study maps and drive round the city for about two years. Before they can start driving people, they have to answer difficult questions about the best ways across London.

You can move across London on the Underground, too. Londoners also call these underground trains 'the Tube'. The London Underground is the oldest in the world. People first used it in 1863. Now it is about 410 kilometres long. There are three hundred stations, and some of them are nearly sixty metres under the streets. Every day, about 2,500,000 people use these trains.

The Map Man

In 1931, Henry Beck started working on a new map for the London Underground. He wanted to make the map easy for people. The London Underground only made five hundred of the maps, but people loved them. The Underground is bigger today, but the map is not very different from Beck's map.

You can, of course, walk round London! No cars or buses can go across London's newest bridge. The Millennium Bridge opened in 2000, and many Londoners walk across it every day. There were some problems with the bridge in the early days. When a lot of people walked on it, the bridge moved! People felt ill, so the bridge had to close. Builders did more work on the bridge, and then it opened again.

London between the Pages

London is a great city for book-lovers. There are a lot of bookshops on Charing Cross Road. Many famous writers lived in – and wrote about – the city.

Samuel Pepys (1633–1703) wrote about life in the city in the 1600s. His work tells us about the Great Fire of London in 1666.

Dr Samuel Johnson (1709–84) wrote about the English language and many other things. Johnson wrote these famous words about his home city: 'When a man is tired of London, he is tired of life.'

Jane Austen (1775–1817) lived in London for a short time. She loved to go shopping in Bond Street.

Charles Dickens (1812–70) was the most famous writer in Victorian England (when Victoria was queen). Many of his books are about London. When Dickens was a child, his family had no money. He had to work. Later, he wanted to make the city a better place. In his book *Oliver Twist*, young Oliver has a very bad time on the streets of Victorian London.

Arthur Conan Doyle (1859–1930) wrote the first Sherlock Holmes story in 1891 and he gave the great detective an address in the city. There really is a 221b Baker Street. There is also a Sherlock Holmes museum in the street.

George Bernard Shaw (1856–1950) lived in a house in Bloomsbury. Later, Virginia Woolf lived in the same house. E M Forster and many other writers met at this house.

George Orwell (1903–1950) wrote his most famous book, *1984*, about a London of the future. Orwell also wrote about difficult lives in the city in his book *Down and Out in London and Paris*.

Sherlock Homes looks up to his old home in Baker Street.

Martin Amis (born 1949) gives a good picture of London life in the 1980s in his book *Money*. London is important in a lot of his books.

Zadie Smith (born 1973) wrote about the lives of British Asians in London now in her book *White Teeth*. London is always changing, and today's writers show readers the new faces of the city.

Many famous books for children are about London. In J M Barrie's book, Peter Pan flies over the buildings of London. In P L Travers's book, Mary Poppins also flies over London!

Sports

It doesn't always rain in Britain! When the weather is good, what can Londoners do outside? The city has more than 1,700 parks. About 30% of the city is parks and green areas. The biggest park in the centre of the city is Hyde Park. You can walk round it in about ninety minutes. You can also take a boat out on the water.

You can watch sports in London, too.

- Every June, sports-lovers watch the tennis at Wimbledon. This brings the top tennis players in the world to the city.
- In March or April, boats from Cambridge and Oxford Universities try to be the fastest on the River Thames. Students come to London and watch with Londoners.
- Football is the biggest sport in Britain. Arsenal, Chelsea, West Ham and Tottenham Hotspur play in London.

◆

London is a city with many faces. It is home to some of the world's richest people, to kings and queens, and to people with little or no money. There are old buildings and new buildings. You can eat English food all day or you can eat food from other countries. There are a lot of cars, a lot of shops – and a lot of people. Life in London is not always easy, but it is never boring. Dr Johnson was right: 'When a man is tired of London, he is tired of life.'

ACTIVITIES

Pages 1–7

Before you read

1 What do you know about London? Write the names of:
   a two buildings   **c** a football ground
   b a street   **d** an airport

2 Look at the Word List at the back of the book. Then discuss these questions with another student.
   a How many kings and queens of Britain can you name?
   b Name a famous work of art. Do you like it? Why (not)?
   c In your area, are there more new or old buildings? Which do you like more?
   d You are in London for one day. Are you going to visit a museum or see a play? Why?
   e What is the capital city of your country? Why is that city the capital?
   f Is there a street market near your home? What can you buy there?

While you read

3 Are these questions right (✔) or wrong (✘)?
   a London is the biggest city in the world.   .....
   b The River Thames is north of London.   .....
   c People from London are Londonians.   .....
   d One old London Bridge is in California.   .....
   e There are no fish in the Thames now.   .....
   f The Romans went to England.   .....
   g Vikings built a new London Bridge.   .....
   h Most of the big theatres are in the East End.   .....
   i Early in the 1600s, London theatres were only outside the city walls.   .....
   j William Shakespeare lived in London.   .....

25

After you read

4 Answer these questions.

   a How many bridges are there in London?

   b When did the Romans arrive in Britain?

   c When did they leave?

   d Why did Boudica destroy most of London?

   e Who built the second Westminster Abbey?

   f Who built the first London theatre?

5 Discuss these questions with another student.

   a Why was the River Thames important to London?

   b Was the new Globe Theatre a good idea? Would you like to go there? Why (not)?

Pages 8–15

Before you read

6 Discuss these questions.

   a What do you know about the Queen's home in London?

   b How many different languages do you think you can hear in London? Why?

   c Something destroyed most of London in the 1600s. What do you think it was?

While you read

7 Who:

   a lost their heads in the Tower of London?   ....

   b lost his palace and his life?   ....

   c lives in Buckingham Palace?   ....

   d was born in Kensington Palace?   ....

   e are born near the sound of Bow Bells?   ....

   f tried to destroy the government in 1605?   ....

   g built St Paul's Cathedral?   ....

   h was Queen Victoria's husband?   ....

   i lost at Trafalgar?   ....

8 Read about one of the people in 7 (above). Use books or the Internet and write five interesting sentences. Then tell the other students about that person.

9 Work with another student. Have this conversation. Where are you going to go? Why?

Student A: It is your last day in London and you want to visit St Paul's Cathedral. You want your friend to go with you.

Student B: You don't want to visit St Paul's Cathedral. You want to go on the London Eye. You want your friend to go with you.

Pages 16–24

Before you read

10 Who or what are these? What do you know about them?
  a Harrods
  b the London Underground
  c Charles Dickens
  d Mary Poppins
  e Wimbledon
  f Arsenal

While you read

11 Write the date.
  a Fortnum & Mason opened. ....
  b Harrods was the biggest shop in Europe. ....
  c The British Museum opened. ....
  d People found the Lindow Man. ....
  e The first Tate museum opened. ....
  f People first used the Underground. ....
  g Jane Austen died. ....
  h Conan Doyle first wrote about Sherlock Holmes. ....

After you read

12 What did Dr Johnson say about London? What did he mean? Can you say the same words about your town or city? Why (not)?

13 Look at the questions on page 1 again. Can you answer all of them now?

Writing

14 You are going to London for two days. What do you want to see and do? Make a plan.

15 You are on holiday in London. Write a postcard to a friend at home. What do you think about the city?

16 The year is 1610. Today, you saw a new play by Shakespeare. Write about your day.

17 In a magazine, you read about 'The Five Greatest Cities in the World'. London is not there. Write a letter to the magazine about this.

18 You are a teacher. Tell your students, on paper, some of the story of London. Use words and pictures.

19 You are making a film about 'the new face of London'. What will you show? Make notes for your film.

A Great City page 1: Answers

1b   2a   3c   4b   5b   6a   7c   8a   9b   10a